Winning

Crappie

Secrets

Revised Edition

by
Tim Huffman

published by:
Huffman Publishing
PO Box 26
Poplar Bluff, MO 63902
www.monstercrappie.com

Printed in USA by:
　　　　Corning Publishing
　　　　810 N. Missouri Ave.
　　　　Corning, AR 72422

ISBN number: 0-9654766-0-X

Cover: Ronnie Capps and Steve Coleman display fish from a winning stringer caught at Kentucky Lake.

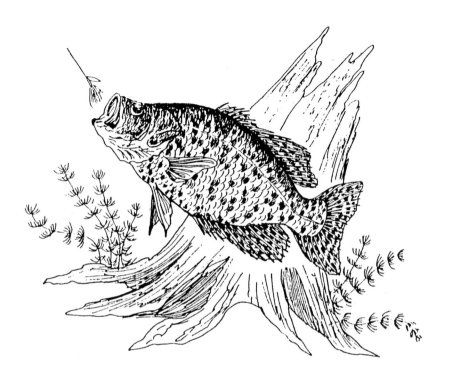

Huffman Publishing
Outdoor Education & Entertainment

Table of Contents

Dedication

You have gone further to reach your goals than most fishermen could ever imagine. You have won three Classics, so far. You have taken crappie fishing to a new level. I dedicate this book to you, Ronnie and Steve, for being different, for your relentless pursuit of excellence and then sharing all of your information with others to help make them better fishermen.

Why a New Revised Edition?

First, all copies have sold from the original printing.

Two, Ronnie and Steve often tell me of changes and improvements in their system. I've included their newest concepts mixed with the time-tested information provided in the first edition.

Therefore, the purpose has been to get another book to the printer with the most current tips to help you in your fishing. I hope this serves as a guide for your slow vertical trolling.

Chapter 1

Boats & Rigging

-Checklist
-Boats for Slow Trolling
-Seating
-Accessories

Boats and Rigging

Your boat for slow trolling should be one that fits your needs. It should be comfortable, safe and efficient. Your boat may not be good for my fishing; or my boat for yours.

Checklist

The size and rigging of a boat is usually based upon three basic things. They are (in order): cost and affordability; the right size for home water; and seriousness of fishing.

The order for selecting a boat is a little different. First, it should be the right size for the water to be fished. If you only fish ponds and very small lakes, a small jon boat will be easier to handle. It can be slid down a bank where no launching ramp is available. However, this boat is not practical or safe for big water.

Seriousness in catching fish is another important factor. A high-performance glass boat may be the right choice. A fiberglass boat with a big engine will get from spot to spot in a hurry, be a stable fishing platform and provide the most safety. A serious fisherman will carefully rig all accessories for maximum efficiency and comfort.

The third factor is cost. A low priced boat isn't worth a dime if you can't properly fish from it. Therefore, select a boat style and then look for the best price. The good thing about slow vertical trolling is that almost any type boat can be used and the rigging doesn't have to be expensive. There's nothing wrong with not having a lot of money, it's just a little inconvenient at times. Careful planning and buying can keep costs to a minimum.

Rigging can be very basic or extensive depending on your preference. Match your budget, home water and level of fishing to your choice of rigging. Above all, take time to do it right.

Boats for Slow Trolling

Ronnie has used a small canoe on Reelfoot Lake to quickly get from spot to spot for checking stumps. A small engine and a few rod holders makes this a simple, effective rig for prefishing tournaments and fun fishing. The team even won a tournament in 1996 fishing from a canoe. However, a canoe is very limited because of winds and waves so it's not practical for a primary boat.

A small jon boat is light and easy to handle. A small jon is good for ponds, small impoundments and stump-filled waters. The size and type of boat is not a limiting factor to catching fish. However, it must provide full control for the conditions.

An ultra-long boat isn't recommended for slow trolling, but proves that you can use almost any boat for this technique. This is at a Classic when their primary fiberglass boat was having problems.

The small boat's enemy is wind and waves. A small boat must be used where waves won't be a problem. This may require selecting the right fishing days or fishing areas with good wind breaks. Dangerous situations must be avoided.

A mid-sized aluminum bass boat and a small fiberglass

boat are very good rigs for slow trolling. Setups using these boats allow a lot of flexibility in rigging. They are the most versatile for fishing all types of waters.

Large aluminum and mid-sized fiberglass boats are excellent for slow trolling. They have more room for seating, poles and equipment. Serious fishermen usually have one of these two boats because they offer most of the required characteristics needed at a lower price than the deluxe fiberglass boats. Their only disadvantages are price and heavier pulling weight.

A serious tournament fisherman needs a large fiberglass boat. Large boats have room, weight and provide safety. Room and safety are obvious advantages. Space for rods, tackle and equipment improves efficiency and enjoyment. Safety allows rougher water to be traveled and fished.

A lot of weight is the opposite of what most people want in a boat but it can be advantageous. Weight improves stability. Weight control will be detailed later in this book.

Another advantage of a large boat is speed. The quicker a fisherman can travel, the more time he can fish.

Large pontoon boats have lot of space and can be used for this method. They are, however, the least desirable of all boats. Control is a problem because they catch a lot of wind. With boat control being critical, they're limited to calm days and areas protected from bad winds.

Seating

Most 'bass' boats are rigged with a front deck pedestal seat. This is fine for one-person fishing and can be totally rigged accordingly. However, slow trolling is particularly suited to two-person fishing. A few modifications are required for most boats to accommodate this style. They include the following.

(1) Fishing in front is the obvious choice when fishing alone. All controls and poles are situated to be fished from the front.

(2) Fishing two in the front has many advantages. All poles are close to the structure being viewed on the trolling motor transducer. In normal fishing and with fishermen in front and back, one fisherman's poles may never get closer than 30 feet to a brush

pile or stump where the majority of fish are located. This situation is obviously not as efficient as two in the front.

Another big advantage of fishing from the front is teamwork. It's easy to swap trolling motor control, watch each other's poles and dip fish with a landing net. Both fishermen are in control and in the strike zone.

The Capps/Coleman team takes advantage of two-in-front fishing because it improves their effectiveness. To achieve this setup, they added two bases, pedestals and seats to the front deck.

They recommend the following ideas if you add two seats in front. Move the seats and rack as far forward as possible to get poles away from the boat. The only disadvantage of having two seats in front is crowding; pay close attention to distances and seat size (good reason for bicycle type seats.)

Ronnie says in a 2003 interview, "Today we fish almost exclusively from the front of the boat. The reason is we're using fewer poles. We can be more precise about putting the bait where it needs to be. We can keep the front of the boat where we want it to be but the back end likes to run around a lot with the wind."

(3) Fishing isn't always best from just the front. One in front and one in back can be an advantage in several situations. First, when winds are too strong to fish effectively in front, the back of the boat is more stable. One person can fish out of the back on good structure while the front fisherman controls the boat (and probably doesn't catch fish).

Another situation is when pole limits are six or more per person. Fishing from the back and front allows more poles. Ronnie and Steve fish as many as 26 poles; 10 in front and 16 in back.

Although this is productive it's very hard work and requires much practice.

Decks are another factor in boat selection and seating. Dropped front decks are becoming more popular because they are safer. A fisherman isn't as likely to fall overboard from a dropped deck. Another advantage is that a dropped deck is warmer in the winter. For most crappie fishing situations, a dropped deck is a positive feature.

Dropped decks require a boat that's a little wider if two are fishing in the front. Knees or shins will hit the sides if the boat is too narrow. Also, the dropped deck doesn't allow the storage underneath that a raised deck gives.

Accessories

Three items needed for slow vertical trolling are electronics, trolling motor and rod holders. A locator is necessary to quickly find potential hotspots. The type of locator used is a matter of personal preference providing it's a quality unit.

In 2003 Ronnie says, "Lowrance is still the best equipment in my opinion. The X65 and X75 are good and the X15 is wonderful. I've got a 1600 GPS."

"When we first talked to you about this book I believe it was in 1996. We were doing some strange stuff then trying to do the best job possible at finding structure. Locators today have made that job easy. I believe our cone angle is up to 23 or 26 degrees now instead of 16 degrees. The electronics is so much better now than five or six years ago. More pixels give better readouts. They're more sensitive with liquid crystal being about as good as the paper graph recorders with much less problems."

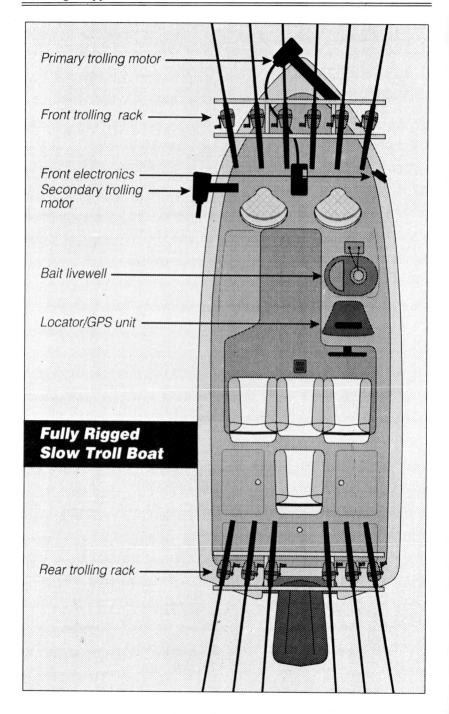

Primary trolling motor

Front trolling rack

Front electronics
Secondary trolling
motor

Bait livewell

Locator/GPS unit

**Fully Rigged
Slow Troll Boat**

Rear trolling rack

A trolling motor is the heart and soul of slow trolling. The bigger the better when it comes to trolling motor power. Variable speed and plenty of power are the most important characteristics. Quiet, easy operation is also critical. "We run the biggest we can. That's a Minn Kota 101 foot controlled motor. I didn't want all the other bells and whistles that can cause more breakdowns. The more dependable the better."

I remember Ronnie talking about going through two sets of batteries (four batteries) during a day of fishing in the wind. *Doesn't the bigger thrust cause a lot of problems with batteries?* "The newer motors are more energy efficient and have a 36 volt system. I can run all day."

The third item, pole holders, may be a new idea to some fishermen. Pole holders are required to fish multi-pole techniques. They allow you to work with one pole at a time, complete other chores, yet safely hold poles and baits in the strike zone.

Pole holders come in many shapes and sizes. Two primary brands dominate the crappie fishing market at this time. One is the Driftmaster Lit'l Pro series with the associated rack. The second is Tite-Lok holders. The Black Widow Ultra with holders is Tite-Lok's premier trolling system in 2003. The key is to have a holder that's easy to get the pole out of with a straight up hookset.

Pole holders can be fastened directly to a boat or mounted on a rack. A rack has the advantage of placing all holders in close proximity to one another at an equal height. Bites are easier to see and poles are accessible.

Homemade racks were standard in the past. At the first printing of this book, they still totally dominated because they could be made to fit at specific heights, lengths or other necessary criteria. Today things have changed. Better racks that do a good job are available.

"We've switched to Tite-Lok pole holders," says Ronnie. "They're a lot better now. The company has come a long way to improve the stability of their racks. The beefed-up system does a good job for our slow trolling and even pulling crankbaits."

Other Details

Boat setup includes organization: a place to put poles; a handy place for the net; an area for tackle boxes; etc. An organized boat makes everything automatic so no thinking is required. For example, you turn to your right to get bait out of the minnow bucket. It's always there and handy. Move the bucket and you have to look for it.

Another example is the landing net. When a big fish is on, you should be able to grab the landing net handle without looking for it. The net should be kept in the same location all of the time and care should be taken that nothing gets placed where it will tangle with the net. (There's nothing like having a slab on the line, grabbing the net handle and having three reels tangled in the net laying on the floor.)

Clean is nice, too. But don't confuse clean with organized.

Tackle should be kept to a minimum. Slow vertical trolling requires line, sinkers, hooks, swivels and a few jigs. It's relatively simple. Don't take three tackle boxes full of junk. Stick to good basics.

Tournament fishermen need to pay close attention to details. Keeping everything working and in good condition is important.

Fishing in front and back offers several advantages. When pole limits are liberal or non-existent, it's possible for each fisherman to rig 8 to 16 poles each. The more practical method is to fish side-by-side using six to ten long poles.

Summary
Chapter 1 Boats and Rigging

>Boat selection should depend upon: cost and affordability; the right size for home water; and seriousness of fishing.

>Two people in the front is the best way to keep all baits in the strike zone area and to work together when fish are biting.

>Quality electronics are critical. A good locator will show you what's under the water. A GPS lets you get to where you're going and more importantly, to get back to the exact spot at a later date.

>Pole holders are an important tool to manage multiple poles. Check to find what is available to best suit your specific needs.

>A rack is the best way to control holders. Again, match your needs to what you put onto your boat.

Chapter 2

Finding the Right Spot

-Maps
-Locators

Finding the Right Spot

There are no guarantees in crappie fishing. Fish move, water conditions change and some days the fish just don't bite. Two items can guarantee that you have all the odds in your favor every time you go fishing. These are not the combination of dynamite and matches, but rather something legal...a map and a locator.

Maps

A good topo map can let you find the best potential locations before going to a lake. The best spots on unfamiliar water are often areas similar to the successful locations on your home lake. Your experience and knowledge will play a big factor selecting the right spots.

Some waters have no contour maps available. Your best option is to get on the lake and visualize what the contour and depths should be by the slope of the bank. Points, creek inlets, bluffs and other contours are obvious. By selecting an area and thoroughly checking it with your locator, you can pinpoint the 'best bet' spots.

Most large waters have contour maps. These maps range from excellent to very poor. The poor ones have no contour lines.

The map is simply a guide to the lake. Spend a few extra dollars and get the best.

Good maps have contour lines that show points, ledges, etc. The separation or closeness of lines indicate the slope of the bottom. Close lines indicate a sharp drop-off while lines that are far apart show a slight slope or flat. Ronnie and Steve often use a Geological survey map. They also like Fishing HotSpot maps because they are waterproof and tear resistant.

Ronnie and Steve closely study a map before going to a lake. "To me, a creek ledge is the best structure for crappie," says Ronnie. "The season doesn't matter. We look for something different. A leading edge of a ledge is a good place to start. Points, a jut (cut) or anything that varies or is different are good places to mark on a map."

The Capps/Coleman team have many examples proving that their selection of locations are successful ones. The 1995 Classic in Ohio had teams fishing for shallow, spawning crappie. The team wanted to catch spawning fish, too, but they went to deep water on a ledge. They caught white crappie that were black in color. Fish were spawning at 18 to 20 feet in the clear water.

Another example of pre-selecting locations happened at Lake Conway, Arkansas. Ronnie and Steve won the tournament by fishing the deepest water in the shallow lake. Conway is filled with stumps, but the team found a deep water spot that had some of the biggest stumps in the lake. That 'something different' gave them depth, a ledge and a magnet for crappie. It all started with a contour map of the lake and pre-selecting the right spot.

In another tournament, the team set a Crappiethon one-day record for that time with 10 fish weighing over 18 pounds. They

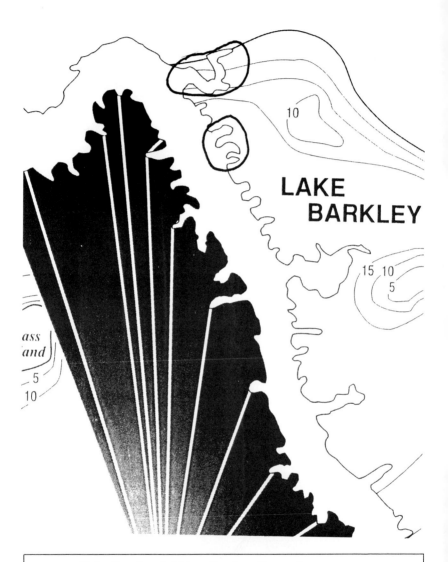

Selecting the right location is a three-step process.

Step 1. Select an Area

It may be a creek, a large cove, the main river channel or open water structure. In our example, we want to fish on the northern end of the lake. For the season, creeks should be a prime target. The contour map can be checked to see if the major creek or smaller bays we've marked have a good depth range.

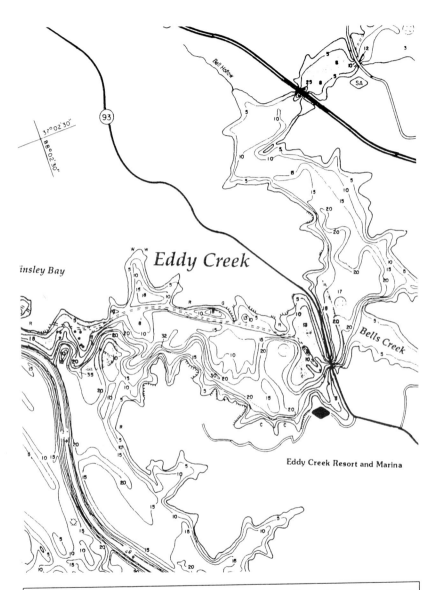

Eddy Creek

insley Bay

Eddy Creek Resort and Marina

Step 2. Select a Major Location (or several) to Check for Fish
We'll choose the big creek we marked on the previous page.
It's Eddie Creek; a popular bass and crappie location on Barkley. The
creek is exceptional because all of its fishable water in the 8 to 20 foot
range.

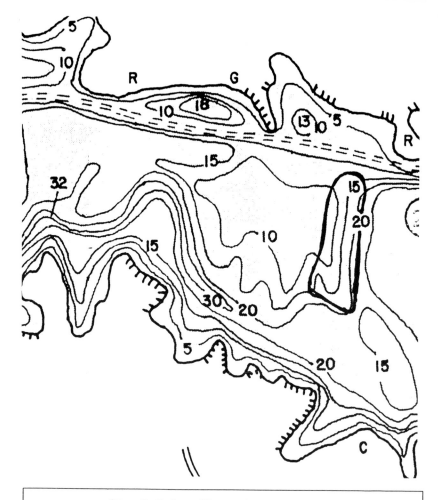

Step 3. Select 'Something Different'

It's not clear-cut on this creek because of all the excellent structure: channel bends, cuts, points, flats, humps, sharp drops, mild drops and depressions. Most creeks will have only three or four of these features making selection easier.

There are no definite right or wrong choices. We'll select a drop next to 20 foot water off a 10-foot flat. The southern end has a good point, there's a consistent ledge toward the north, ending with an outside channel bend.

There are plenty other structures that may be better and can be tried. The point of the drawing is to select something specific; have a purpose and a goal. Don't just randomly fish.

were fishing a point in deep water in a creek arm of Kentucky Lake. On the map, the point is extremely narrow at a depth of 15 to 18 feet falling immediately to 30 feet. They used a map and then locators to find the point. They caught big fish.

Steve has a practical way of looking at channels, ledges and points. "A creek channel can be thought of as a main road. Inlets or intersections are secondary roads. Just like people, fish follow these natural paths. An intersection is always a potential spot for crappie."

Once an area is marked on the map, an on-the-water search with a locator pinpoints areas to fish. The team seldom uses marker buoys but recommends them when fishing an unfamiliar area. They can be pulled in as soon as a position is triangulated.

To find areas that you've marked on a map, use landmarks for coordinates. Points, covers and other spots can be used on the map and on the water. For example, if a ledge in open water is the target, use landmarks on the map to draw coordinates. Lining a point on one bank with a point on the other can give a line that intersects the ledge. By following the drawn line in a boat while watching the locator, the ledge can be found.

A second tip is to note cover. While scouting with a locator, mentally mark (or use a buoy) any stumps, brush piles or other cover that's unique to the ledge. The cover can be a fish magnet, especially if associated with the drop.

Third: Watch for fish. Although this is the least important step, heavy concentrations of fish indicate their presence and primary depth.

Fourth: Bottom hardness. Ronnie and Steve admit that bottom hardness is a key for finding fish. It's overlooked by most fishermen, but it shouldn't be. Fishing experience and underwater diving has taught the team its importance. A good locator will indicate hardness by the width (strength of the return). Be sure to pay attention.

Now, maybe the most important tip this chapter; don't quit looking until you find the area you've marked on the map. Search the area for your marked structure, look for surrounding cover, check for bottom hardness and the presence of fish. Learn where you are and where you want to be. Time spent looking for a spot

Locator Tips

Your locator probably came with a simulation mode. Use it while you're at home with the operator's manual in front of you. Use all of the controls to see what they do to the screen.

Buttons are on a locator for a reason. Learn to take the unit off of 'automatic' so you can find the best settings for your fishing.

Key buttons you should use include: depth; gain (sensitivity); contrast, bottom lock; zoom.

What about cone angles? A wide cone angle of 20-degrees or more is good for finding scattered fish and cover. However, in deeper water you may be many feet away from the fish you're seeing.

A narrow cone angle makes it easy to miss seeing cover and fish, but if you do see them you have them located under your transducer. Therefore, a narrow cone angle is better for pinpointing specific cover and fish.

is much more productive than looking for it while fishing a dead area.

2003 fact: "There is so much stuff out with GPS that maps are available within the GPS units. These are often better than what you can buy," says Ronnie.

Locators

A weekend or recreational fisherman can use any type of flasher or crystal unit. The number one requirement is to find a ledge or contour change. Any locator will do that job.

Seeing fish, brush and bottom hardness are other requirements. Different locators will display this in different ways. Sensitivity and resolution are two locator characteristics that will determine the amount of information shown. The quality of the locator is often directly related to price.

Serious fishermen and tournament pros may want more elaborate units and setups. A wide screen, side transducer, scanning transducer and multi-element transducer provides more detail information.

Is more information critical to success? No. The advantage of more information is speed. Time is important when fishing. Better locator systems can provide more fish by reducing the time required to find structure.

Ronnie and Steve use quality Lowrance depthfinders. The team says high resolution has turned average fishermen into a very good fishermen, especially when matched with a good GPS unit.

Another element that's very important to the team is to locate all structure along a 100 to 500 foot section of ledge before starting to fish. The team throws a marker or finds landmarks on the bank. They go back and fish the located structures.

"Selecting the right spot on the map, going to it on the water and fishing it effectively takes practice," says Steve. "Just like anything else you do, the more you do it the better you'll be. There is no substitute for experience."

GPS

A new item in full use is the GPS unit. The team uses theirs for lake contour maps, scouting, fishing, marking potential locations, marking proven spots and for navigation. In their opinion, every serious fisherman must have one of these units.

"GPS is important for getting to the winners circle," says Ronnie. "It's been a disadvantage for us because of our ability to locate stuff initially and to go back to the exact spot. Other fishermen couldn't always do that. Now, anybody can punch a button and go back to the same place. We've lost a little steam because of the ability of competition to do the same thing with GPS that we were doing ten years ago with good notes and hard work. Average fishermen are right with us now on their ability to do these things."

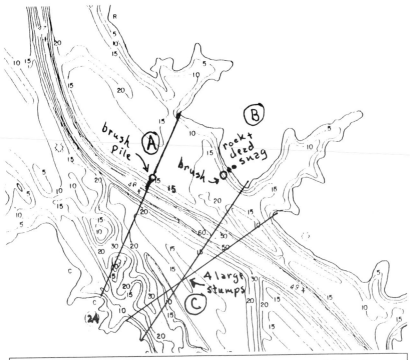

Finding a spot is a simple matter of aligning items and following a path between them until they intersect another line. Don't hesitate to mark top locations on your map for future reference.

A. Follow the 15-foot contour until you intersect with a line drawn from the two points.

B. Cover close to shore can be found by aligning two items on shore. In this example a rock and dead snag. Align the two items then go to the correct depth.

C. With no sharp drop-off, intersecting lines must be used to pinpoint the large stumps in open water.

Summary
Chapter 2 Finding the Right Spot

>*Get the best topo (contour) map available for the lake.*

>*Pre-mark spots to fish before getting on the lake.*

>*Mark good spots you find while fishing.*

>*A quality locator will show more structure, cover and fish.*

>*A GPS turns an average fisherman into a very good one.*

Chapter 3

Equipment

-Poles
-Reels

Equipment

There's nothing like using the right tool for the job. A knife will sometimes work in place of a screwdriver, but the screwdriver offers less slip, more torque and definitely more safety. Likewise, good long poles will work better than shorter poles for slow vertical trolling. They should be a priority on your list of equipment.

The same thing applies to tackle. Don't try to save $1.00 per hundred on hooks by buying regular Aberdeen hooks instead of extra-light wire hooks. Ronnie and Steve have tried almost everything and know what items work best. Pay attention to learn what they use and why a certain type, length and size is preferred. Knowing 'why' makes you a smarter, logical buyer and user.

Poles and Reels

Long poles are super tools for slow trolling. The team's choice for long poles in 2003 is the same as it was six years ago. They have tried other brands and models but have stuck to what works best for them...12-foot BnM jigging poles.

Two very important keys for this technique to work properly are keeping the lines far enough away that they have good separation and to keep them away from the trolling motor. However, lines must be close enough so you can see them.

Long poles keep lines away from the trolling motor and boat. For example, you catch a fish, turn around to drop him into the livewell and a gust of wind blows you sideways off of the spot. Lines are no longer vertical. As lines become more horizontal (parallel to the surface), they can quickly rise into the trolling motor. A good distance keeps them from rising to the motor when the boat is out of control or when speed is used to get from one brush pile to another.

Twelve-foot poles have other advantages including fewer spooked fish. Fish become spooky as water depth decreases and clarity increases. Long poles are important for more bites.

Any pole used for slow vertical trolling must have a reel. Their choice of reel changed a couple of years ago. They previously used spin-cast, also called closed-face reels. They are inexpensive and usually withstand rough treatment. Their disadvantage is that being under

Here's what we hope to catch when we head for the lake. This stringer came from the famous Kentucky Lake.

the long pole they have to be reeled backwards. (Can't put the reel on top because the line will immediately tangle at the end of the pole). Therefore, they are awkward.

Spinning reels work but they have bails to trip and the bails are easily broken in storage and travel. However, the team has switched to the small Mitchell SM200 SpiderMite spinning reels. "We've gotten use to the weight of the reel and we really like them," says Ronnie. "The hookset and handling of the reels are what we've gotten use to using. We keep everything the same because a change in reel weight really changes the 'feel' of the pole for bites and setting the hook."

The team says they wear out several reels because of the time they spend on the water but haven't experienced major problems in breaking bails like they thought would happen. The very small reel has a small bail so it is less susceptible to getting broken.

Line-keeper type reels are okay shallow but are not good when a fish has to be reeled up from deep water.

Many teams have switched to baitcasters. They withstand any abuse and wear that a crappie fisherman will give. Also, they have big handles that are easy to grab and reel.

The team says that reel type isn't critical. What's important is to stay consistent between poles and get comfortable using the reel you choose.

Pole Characteristics

The team uses B&M poles. The following are the characteristics important to these and other poles.

One: 12-foot length keeps line away from the boat yet close enough to see the line.

Two: Reel seat. A good seat prevents a reel from turning and slipping. Slip rings and sticky tape are more aggravation than a permanent seat. However, slip rings allow placement of the reel in any position.

Three: An EVA foam handle. It's a must for Ronnie and Steve's efficiency. They put their double-hook rig's upper hook into a rod eye; the bottom hook goes into the foam handle. It's extremely quick, easy and efficient.

Four: Line guides. Eyes are preferred over wire snake guides. The wire keeps line next to the pole and causes unwanted friction. Ceramic eyes promote smoother line flow.

Five: Stiffness. A limber rod with some backbone is the best choice. A stiff rod causes baits to bounce with every little up and down movement of the boat. Limber rods absorb the shock which helps to stabilize the baits.

Woops!! Wrong fish to be catching while slow trolling for crappie. Gar, catfish, bass and drum are very common catches while easing baits through feeding areas. These 'trash fish' can put a big bend in a long pole.

Six: Sensitivity. Ronnie and Steve want to see that the minnows are active. A sensitive rod can show every small bump, movement and the first indication of a strike.

Here's a quick tip that can help your long poling. Long trips beat poles together creating wear and rough places that cause line to stick to the pole. The team uses Armour-All to smooth the poles so line will slide better and not hang up. Also, Reel Magic by Blakemore is a convenient, spray that will do the same job.

Summary
Chapter 3 Poles and Reels

>*Key to a reel for slow trolling is: ability to reel, easy to use.*

>*The right pole is important. See chapter text for specific characteristics.*

>*Tip: keep poles clean and slick to avoid line sticking.*

Chapter 4

Rigs for Minnows and Jigs

-The Basic Rig
-Rig Components
-Advanced Rigs

Reel - mithell Sm 200 Spidermite
Pole - 13ςm 12' Limber w/ Backbone
        Foam Handle
Line - 10 lb.

Rigs for Minnows and Jigs

A minnow or jig can be rigged in many different ways to catch crappie. The rig discussed here will be the Capps & Coleman rig. It has been tried, changed, modified, improved and proven. The rig has been successful in Florida, Ohio and many waters in between.

An advantage of this rig is that the minnows and jigs are rigged identical. Setup is easy because components, line lengths and characteristics are the same.

The rig and components description are detailed in the following text. It's important to understand the basic rig. Once understood, it can be modified to fit each specific fishing situation.

The Basic Rig

(1) The main line is tied to the top of a three-way swivel.

(2) A four foot length leader is tied to the bottom of the swivel.

(3) An egg sinker is tied on the leader 18 inches below the swivel.

(4) A hook or jig is tied 12 inches below the sinker.

(5) A 12-inch leader is tied to the side eye of the three-way swivel.

(6) A hook or jig is tied to the 12-inch leader

That's it. A versatile, effective fish-catching system. The basic rig can be made longer, shorter, lighter or heavier with no significant change in design.

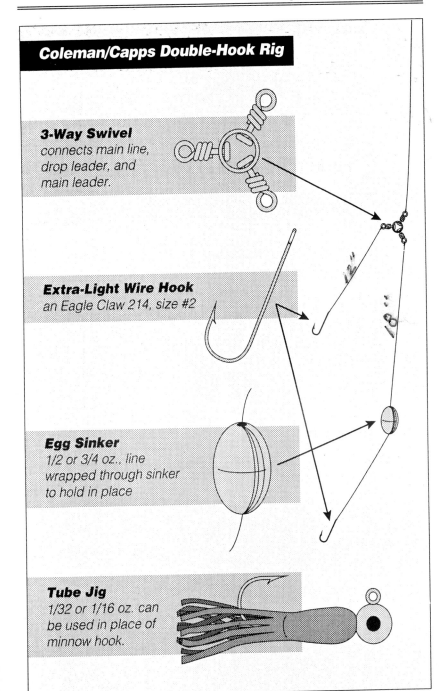

Coleman/Capps Double-Hook Rig

3-Way Swivel
connects main line,
drop leader, and
main leader.

Extra-Light Wire Hook
an Eagle Claw 214, size #2

Egg Sinker
1/2 or 3/4 oz., line
wrapped through sinker
to hold in place

Tube Jig
1/32 or 1/16 oz. can
be used in place of
minnow hook.

Rig Components

(1) The reel should be spooled with 10-lb test line. A heavier 12-lb line can be used but it will have more drag resistance in deep water. A lighter 8-lb test line is good but breaks easier. The best choice is 10-lb test because it is stronger than the hooks and leaders. Breaks will occur below the swivel.

(2) Leaders from the three-way swivel are 6 or 8-lb test limp line. Berkley is an excellent choice for the leaders. The long leader should be 8-lb test except in clear water when 6 or 4 is required. The long leader must carry the sinker and bait. It's also the most susceptible part of the rig to hang up. The short leader can be 6 or 8-lb test.

(3) Knots can be your personal choice. Ronnie an Steve use a clinch knot all of the time. It's what they like and can tie quickly.

(4) Swivel. A number 6 or 8 is the best size. A swivel that's too small will cause line problems. A large swivel has too much line drag in deep water situations.

(5) An egg sinker is the best in-line choice. A basic minnow rig uses a 1/2-ounce sinker. This is enough weight to keep the baits down during average fishing conditions.

Fishing shallow water requires shorter rigs and smaller sinkers. A 3/8-ounce is good in shallow water.

Deep water and windy conditions can cause boat control problems and bouncing baits. A 3/4-ounce sinker helps keep baits still and in place.

Deep water conditions can cause a few unique situations where larger weight can be used. We'll discuss big weights near the end of this chapter.

Jig rigs use a slightly lighter weight because of the extra weight of the jig heads. A 3/8-ounce egg in combination with two 1/32-ounce heads is right for all but extreme conditions.

Tying eggs to the line is easy. Simply wrap the line through the sinker four or five times. The wraps will hold a sinker without pegging or tying a knot.

Sinker smoothness is important. A rough edge or burr will cut small line. Buy good eggs.

Tip: Always start your line in the small hole of an egg. Line will come out of the big hole much easier than out of the small hole because of the way they are poured.

Tip: When you hang-up on a bush or stump, just back up and shake the sinker. The sinker will usually pop the hook free.

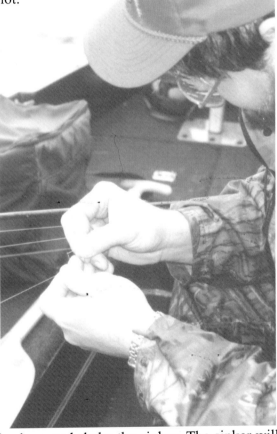

(6) Any style hook will catch a crappie, but some hooks are better than others. The ol' standby for crappie is the #1/0

Aberdeen. It has a lighter wire than a standard hook and a big gap between the hook point and shank. This makes the hook moderately easy to bend when hung in a limb.

Today things have changed. "We use only one type hook," says Ronnie. "It's an Eagle Claw 214; an extra-light, Lazer Sharp, size #2, bronze color. The hook size coupled with the size minnow we use gives us maximum action. There's enough hook there to catch what we're after."

The 'EL' on the Eagle Claw stands for extra-light wire. An extra-light hook will bend even with 8-lb test line when an average Aberdeen would cause the line to break.

Another important feature of the light wire is more minnow action. The small #2 extra-light hook on a long leader will let the minnow swim around and attract crappie. A #1/0 Aberdeen is too big for a minnow to have maximum movement.

Hook sharpness is also important. The Lazer Sharp gives the edge that is needed. A sharp hook penetrate fast which means more caught fish. The disadvantage is that the point bends easily. Tip: Pay attention to the point. Straighten it with your fingernail when it gets bent. The result will be more fish hooked.

Jig hooks are important, too, but the size and type of hooks available are limited. For example, a 1/32-ounce jig normally has a #6 hook. If you prefer a bigger #4 hook like Ronnie and Steve, you must search for a 1/32-ounce head with the right hook size. If you can't find one, you may have to order a mold and make your own.

Advanced Rig Ideas

"We've tried to create a rig as light as possible for maximum bait action. It's an ultra-light compared to the heavy line double-hook, double-loop minnow rigs. Those double loop rigs have more weight, less action and are more visible," says Ronnie.

The team changes line weekly when fishing every day. During tournament season, they change the night before a tournament.

Rigging length is a major variable that's really important to consider. Length depends upon water depth. On Reelfoot Lake in six feet of water, the rig may be two feet long from swivel to lower hook. At Kentucky Lake the rig may be seven feet long.

Tip: Lengthening each drop gives more action and a wider depth range of coverage. The slow movement of the boat keeps the drop away from the main line.

Are fish suspended or on bottom? At the Classic in Ohio the fish were right on bottom. Little wind and a depth of 15 to 18 feet called for a 1/2-ounce sinker and a very short rig to keep both baits on bottom. "It would have been useless to suspend a bait into an unproductive zone."

The exact opposite of the above example is when fish are staggered at different depths. A wide spread will improve odds of putting a bait in front of a fish.

Moral: Adjust for the conditions and situation. Remember the average, common rig dimensions and adjust from there. Swivel to egg is 18 inches; egg to bottom hook is 12 inches; top hook to swivel is 12 inches.

In 2003

The team has been amazed at the popularity of their rig since this book's first printing. "It has definitely taken hold and is being used all over the country," says Ronnie.

Steve agrees but says that the reason is simple. "It's real hot and my belief is that it's still the number one way to catch crappie. People use it because it works."

They emphasize that slow is still the key in most situations but they have learned that other times they can trigger more strikes by speeding up. Ronnie says, "It's the same rig but we've gone to a little heavier weights so can move around a little quicker. I've learned that in some situations the heavier weight don't cut down on strikes. The advantage is that I can cover more ground."

"The 1/2-ounce weight has been our best all-around size in 12 to 15-feet where we like to fish. In 18 or 20 feet of water it becomes a really slow game. We couldn't cover enough water."

"At the Pickwick Classic we went to 1-ounce but still wanted to cover more ground in areas along a river bank that didn't have much cover on it. The fish were scattered and would trigger to a fast bait. We had to go to a 2-ounce sinker to keep our baits down."

The team sometimes pre-ties rigs for convenience and speed on the water. Steve says, "We like to keep a few rigs tied. If we're fishing areas down a ledge with a few stumps we won't worry about it. If we're going to hang up and break off a lot we may pre-tie a couple dozen rigs. We just use the rubber holders that Cabela's carry to hold our rigs."

Summary
Chapter 4 Rigs for Minnows and Jigs

>*Basic Capps/Coleman rig is an excellent all-around setup. You can adjust the hook spread or weight to fit conditions.*

>*3/8-ounce weight in shallow water; 1/2-ounce at mid-depths; 3/4 deep; 1 or 2-ounce in special deep situations.*

>*Get un hung by giving a little slack and shaking the sinker.*

>*Keep hooks sharp.*

>*Jigs can be substituted for minnows.*

Chapter 5

Baits

-Minnow and Jig Mini-Course

Baits

Minnow and Jig Mini-Course

Baits of all types will catch crappie. Water clarity, food sources and water temperature will vary fish preference for a particular bait at a particular time. However, most bait principles are the same; presentation and good bait basics are the key elements. This chapter is filled with Ronnie and Steve's bait ideas. With their proven success, you should be able to apply their basics and special tips to your own methods.

Minnows are the bread and butter of the Capps/Coleman team. They catch fish on both minnows and jigs, but they have trouble beating the success of minnows for both number and size of crappie.

Ronnie and Steve have tried almost every type of minnow. Live shad, buffalo, carp and other natural baits have been on their hooks. "The natural baits just aren't worth the trouble," says Ronnie. "Compared to regular minnows, there is very little difference in the numbers of fish caught."

Two keys are important with minnows: size and action. The team uses Rosy Reds (pink minnows), goldfish and golden shiners. It seldom makes a difference in the type as long as the minnows are active.

The size depends upon the lake. For example, at Monroe the crappie are small so they use small 1.5- to 2.0-inch minnows. At the opposite end of the scale, a 3-inch minnow on Kentucky is a medium size.

The average length used by Ronnie and Steve is around 2.5-inches. A little variation is no problem , but for a tournament day they'll size them by culling large and small baits.

Minnows are hooked through the lips or eyes. A lip hook is less likely to work up the shank of the hook and become fouled like hooking through the eyes. Both methods are good; use your personal preference.

Tip: Always hook the minnow's lips as close to the edge as possible without catching too little to cause it to tear out easily.

Shown here are the two primary options for hooking minnows. One is through the eyes and the other is through the lips. Both methods will allow a minnow to be pulled straight in the water without curling the minnow or twisting the line.

The bait will live longer and have more action than one hooked back toward the head.

"Jigs can be any type," says Ronnie. He explains that the ones he and Steve describe are the ones they like and use. "We can't say that they're the best type jig available because we haven't tried them all. However, they are definitely good and productive for us, so we have no reason to switch."

The team uses a 1/32 ounce head with a #4 hook. The hook size and weight are important to them. They match it with a 1.5 inch Lit' Hustler tube for most situations. The regular skirt seems to work fine. If they want to change, they will go to a bigger model or maybe to a Sparkle Scale tube for more flash.

Colors are basic. Red/chartreuse; white/chartreuse; blue/chartreuse are their standard colors for almost any water. Yellow and white might be selected for muddy water, but the basic colors are all that's normally used.

Tipping with minnows is a popular practice, but Ronnie and Steve also use something different. The team likes Berkley Power Baits like the Crappie Sparkle

Scent isn't just for jigs. Berkley Crappie Nibbles will enhance the attracting ability of your minnows. When the bites are difficult to get, try loading your minnow rigs with powerful scent.

Nibbles for more bites and improved efficiency. "It definitely helps when fishing is slow."

What's New - 2003

Minnows are still the bread-and-butter of this team. They work hard to keep baits active and healthy. Size is important so they select them according to the waters they are fishing.

"Minnows are the same," says Ronnie. "It's important to lip hook them to keep everything in line. Don't hook them to far back in the tough part or you'll not have action and it will kill them. Hook too far up in the lips and you'll lose them easily. There is a sweet spot where you have to hook them. There is some practice that goes into learning that spot. If they're not hooked in the right spot the results are bad."

"If we've made a change it's going to just minnows for almost all of our slow trolling. We still use jigs in jigging situations but for trolling we use minnows almost exclusively."

"We've switched to a regular size minnow bucket with pure oxygen on it. I can keep 20 or 30 dozen minnows alive in less

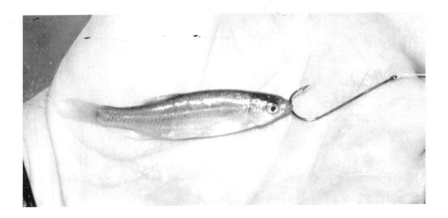

than two gallons of water. They stay good and lively even in the hottest months."

"It's critical to run pure oxygen and put the rock right down in the water. It's easy to move around in the boat. It's a white plastic bucket with the yellow top. Our hose is run into it where it won't come out. We've used it a couple of years now. It gets the job done and doesn't take up a lot of room."

Steve says that every little edge you can gain is an advantage. "We like using the Crappie Nibbles with our minnows. It definitely seemed to help a little at the Pickwick Classic. The Nibbles put enough scent in the water to make the fish bite a little better."

Summary
Chapter 5 ... Baits

>*Jigs for slow trolling should be small to give more action (rig weight is provided by the egg sinker). 1/32-ounce is just right.*

>*Minnows are the top pick for slow trolling. Match the size to the waters fished.*

>*Lip hook minnows so they track straight through the water, have lots of action and live longer.*

Chapter 6

Boat Control

-Basics
-Fishing a Brush Pile

Boat Control

"You must be able to handle poles while maintaining complete boat control.
You must be able to do it all at once; boat control, baiting hooks, catching fish and working with your partner.".....Steve Coleman

The Basics

Execution of the slow vertical trolling technique requires boat control. No other element is more important. Poles can be out of position, baits not quite the right size and line too big but even with those factors some fish will be caught.

Without boat control the speed and location will be wrong. No fish will be caught without good boat speed.

Control begins with speed. Speed remains the same unless an obstacle like a brush top or ledge gets in the way of the baits. The best indication of speed is line angle. A ten to twenty degree line angle with the bait rigs previously described is plenty. It's basically just enough angle to give an indication of movement and direction. Watching line is critical.

Trolling doesn't always stop just because of an obstacle. For example, Ronnie and Steve like to fish into a ledge. While working along a stretch of ledge, baits will be taken into the side of the ledge deliberately. The wind will push them back off.

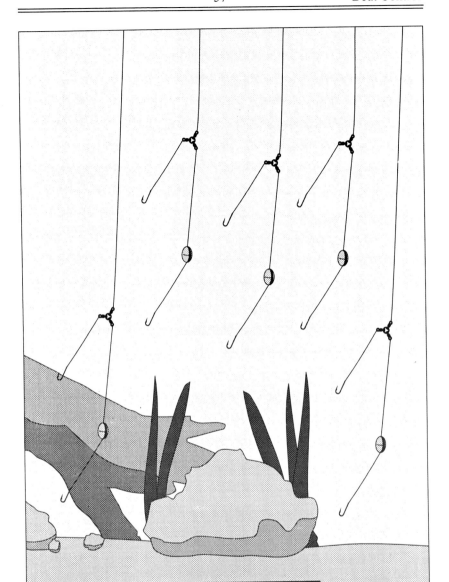

Slow-Trolling Stumps and Brush

Set all but two bait rigs above the cover. The shallow baits will catch crappie located above the cover. The two poles in cover are manageable even when hanging in the cover. These will catch the deeper fish.

Movement doesn't stop unless they want it to. It only changes direction from 'into' the ledge to 'away from' the ledge. The trolling motor is used to control speed into and away from.

Fishing a Brush Pile

The depth fished by Ronnie and Steve depends upon conditions, lake and time of year. It's common to be fishing near the bottom regardless of the depth.

To control depth, they drop baits all the way to the bottom and adjust up. They estimate that one crank on the reel brings the rig up one foot (depends upon the type reel used). Therefore, to fish at 15 feet in 19 feet of water, the bait is dropped to the bottom and reeled up four cranks. (For depth purposes, the team considers the sinker as the bottom of their rig because that's what they can feel bump the cover.)

Questions: Fishing in 15 feet of water with most fish being on bottom, you unexpectedly run into a brush pile that's 4 feet tall in 12 feet of water. How do you fish it?

"I get downwind to start with," says Ronnie. "We drop our baits to the bottom and take one or two cranks. If I'm careless and run into the brush pile, we're hung up bad. We must watch our lines. When the first one hits, I've got to back off. We don't want to hang up and we want to catch the outside fish first. The trolling motor keeps taking us to the brush pile...the wind blows us back."

Steve adds, "By looking at the locator while adjusting baits, a brush pile can be better fished. If we're fishing ten poles, we'll crank six poles to be above the top. Those six are still in the strike zone above the brush and we only have two poles apiece to handle if they get hung up in the brush."

A tip for fishing brush piles or stumps is to fish the edges first. You can ease up to it, catch one and back off of it. You will spook fewer fish and have fewer hangups. After re-baiting, ease back to it. When winds are light, the brush can be approached from different angles.

Fishing inside a brush pile is a last resort, but do it if that's the only way you can catch fish. If you get on top of it, the fish may spook for a while.

Fishing a visible stickup or stump can be a little different. One method is to maintain speed, take the outside pole out of the holder and run the baits around the stump as you pass by. You can stop and fish it if you get a bite.

Another way to fish a stump is by taking the baits directly into the stump, back off slightly, slide them across until all baits are outside, run past the stump with the baits and slide them behind the stump. The stump will end up between the boat and baits. The baits can then be slid back out and trolling continues.

Do you keep moving no matter what?

"Usually, but if we're catching fish at a good brush pile, we might stop there and fish a while. We've got that option with this technique. More than likely, though, we'll be moving back and forth into the brush," says Ronnie.

"We keep saying this, but a good trolling motor is important. Always stay on the control while fishing. We wear out a lot of steering cables. It's not a weak point, we just use it constantly."

A good trolling motor means plenty of power. The team previously used a 24 volt Minn Kota motor. Spare batteries were carried on windy tournament days.

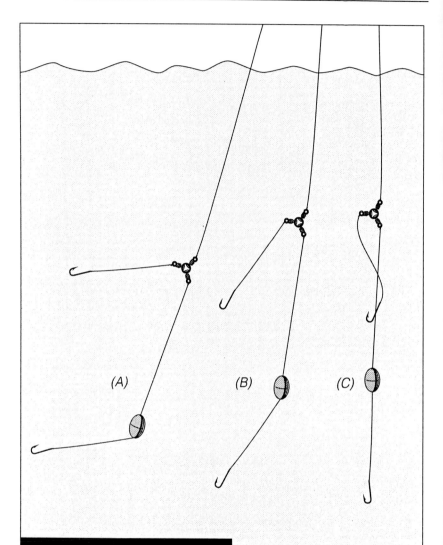

Boat Speed/Line Angle

Line angle is the best indicator of boat speed when slow vertical trolling.

(A) Speed Too Fast: Few bites, baits rise, loss of boat control.
(B) Correct Speed: 10-15 degree line angle is a good speed.
(C) Speed Too Slow: Can't cover enough area, upper hook falls and tangles.

Another feature needed in a trolling motor is quietness. It's not a problem when fishing deep, but shallow fish can spook with very little disturbance like noise. Ronnie and Steve take extra precautions to be as quiet as possible on shallow fish. They have even used a clamp-on trolling motor at the side of the boat to get the motor back another five feet from the fish. Quiet power; not to be ignored for serious fishing.

Bigger Is Better

"Boat control is critical," says Ronnie. "I like to set still. Especially when the water is cold in the winter time. For example, here at Reelfoot people are fishing all around me and not catching fish because they're going too fast. I'm going terribly slow and tearing them up. Others troll right by not catching but one or two fish while I catch a dozen. I'm dragging a chain to slow me down."

"We've gone to the the biggest trolling motor I can run. It's a Minn Kota 101 foot controlled motor and it's 36 volts. We need all the power we can get to stay where we need to be in the wind."

Fishing Shallow

Any special situations where you've slow trolled very shallow water?

"I really got into fish here at Reelfoot in May in the lily pads," says Ronnie. "I was fishing jigs tipped with minnows on 6-lb line. My jigs were probably 8 or 10 inches deep. I had eight poles out the front trolling as slow as I could."

You obviously couldn't use the double-hook rig?

"No weights, just a jig. The fish would see those little jigs bounce off of the lily pad stems and they would hit. You had to move real slow. And it was an area most people wouldn't get into with a trolling outfit. Everybody else stayed on the edges. I went right through the middle of the pads where the fish were located."

Channel Drop-Offs

A drop is one of your top structure targets. How do you know which drop and how do you find it?

Steve says, "The first thing we have to have is a map. The maps that the Army Corps of Engineers puts out is usually the best. They'll show all of the drops and if they're a fast or slow drop."

"The depth we look for depends upon the time of year. In winter it'll be deeper and in spring shallower than normal. Then we'll look for any type of irregularities. We want something different like a spot that sticks out a little or maybe one that dips in. These spots will likely hold a stump or log...and fish."

The team sets up downwind from the area they want to fish. Boat control is definitely a key issue on a drop-off that's usually in open water.

What determines if the spot is good?

"We'll set up and fish. If we catch two big fish off of one spot we'll fish it. You can catch one good fish off of anything. If you catch two or more something is there that holds fish. We'll mark it on GPS so we can return to it anytime we want to."

Any specific cover you like to find?

Steve continues, "I prefer to see a big stump. Big fish seem to like a big stump. A drop that has a scattered stump here and there will usually have more fish than a drop with a lot of stumps."

Summary
Chapter 6   Boat Control

>*Boat control is critical for successful slow trolling.*

>*Go into the wind; not with the wind unless you drag a chain.*

>*You can set bait depth by dropping to the bottom and reeling up a set number of cranks.*

>*Fish brush pile edges first, then toward the middle.*

>*You can take your outside pole and run a bait around a stump within reach at the side.*

>*Keep moving unless you get to a good spot where you're catching fish.*

<u>Chapter 7</u>

The Bite

The Bite

Getting a bite requires doing everything right that has been discussed so far in this book. Seeing the bite is a matter of proper setup and paying attention.

Proper setup includes using the lightest practical bait rig for the situation. Light means more bites. Therefore, 8-lb test line instead of 15 or 20 improves the number of caught fish.

Look at this practical fishing situation. Ronnie and Steve drop the baits to the bottom. Ronnie says, "We always bump the bottom unless the fish are suspended. Most of the time we'll drop to the bottom no matter how much line it takes. We look at the depthfinder. We look at the particular structure such as a brush pile and key in on that structure's height. We'll reel up and adjust from the bottom trying to put the baits right into the top of the structure. It doesn't matter if we get hung up a little; our baits need to be there."

With the baits in position, it's time for a bite. What is the team watching? Pole tips and line. Ronnie and Steve have been fishing together so long that they take a lot of things for granted. Pole positioning is one example. They're amazed at other fishermen they see. Their pole tips are two feet off the water, their tips unequal and no regard for spacing.

They keep poles equally spaced with rod tips off the water about six inches. The spacing, whether using three poles or ten, keeps everything in logical order and separates lines to keep tangling to a minimum. (A line in the trolling motor or a run by a white bass tangling all lines together can ruin a good day!)

Pole tips next to the water prevents wind from whipping lines as badly as a tip two feet from the water. Tips can't be in the water either. Tips and lines must be visible for seeing bites.

Tips are equally spaced and an equal distance from the water. Anything out of position will be quickly noticed. Scanning ten poles is a job; when everything is the same it is much easier to see one out of place when a bite or hang-up happens.

Describing an actual bite is difficult. Soft bites can come in so many different ways. The team gives constant, intense attention to the rod tips and line for an indication of a bite. Although a few bites will be described here, experience and paying attention is the best way to recognize a bite.

A springtime bite is often easy to see. Pole tips plunge into the water on an energetic spring bite. Nothing subtle on days when fish are active. The second most common springtime bite is slack line. Both type bites require immediate lifting of the pole.

Summer bites, especially in middle depths to shallow water, will be a run away from the boat. "A fish going forward in the summer instead of down may have something to do with the thermocline, but I'm not sure. One thing is for sure, you've got to set the hook as soon as the run starts or he'll spit the hook out."

Fall is an 'off and on' time for predicting bites, but it's a good time to fish and watch for a bite pattern.

Winter is probably the best time to crappie fish. There are fewer people on the lake, fish are aggressive and bites are usually strong. Jigs are good to use in the winter but require a quick response from the fisherman when there's a bite.

Experience is needed to know a bite from a limb. On a hang up, the pole will gradually move opposite the direction of the boat. There's no lifting or quick movement. Only experience can give you the knowledge to know which is which when a tip starts to bend.

On a hang up, don't set the hook! When you hit an obstacle, just back up, shake the large sinker and it'll usually come loose.

If an extra-light wire hook stays in a stump, it can be straightened and pulled free. Ninety percent of break-offs occur

Paying close attention and being ready to set the hook are important elements for catching more fish.

when the sinker lodges in the crack of a stump, between rocks or other similar unforgiving places.

One key to getting and seeing bites is patience. Ronnie and Steve have learned several ways to improve catches just by being patient and using practical fishing sense.

The first tip: If fish don't bite in ten minutes, don't think that the jig color is wrong. Pay attention, be patient and give any potential spot thirty or forty minutes. One or two quality fish an hour is fine.

The second tip is to maintain speed control. Ronnie says, "You can't let everything get to you. You run into a treetop and every rig is hung or broke off. You get mad. Your minnows are dying and the motor gets hung on a stump. You turn around to look and spill your Coke. But don't get stressed out! It's time to back up and regroup. Don't lose patience because you will just move too fast and not catch fish."

A third tip is to move from spot to spot with the big motor. Or, fish slowly to the spot. "Don't kick the trolling motor up to two notches and tell yourself that you're fishing; you're not. Don't speed from spot to spot, but maintain slow speed and fish to a spot 100 or 200 yards away. It's common to run into suspended fish while crossing a channel or to find new cover on a ledge."

While we are discussing patience, is it better to stay with a spot that's not producing or move to another area?

"In tournament fishing, set a game plan and stay with it," says Steve. "At times we've gone a couple of hours without a fish, got impatient and talked about making a quick move. Then, suddenly, two poles go down with big slabs."

"It's hard to stay with a spot that's not producing, but it's paid off more for us to stay than to move. Of course there are times we would have been better off to move, but the majority of the time it's better to stay and fish if you have confidence in the spot."

Seeing bites...a matter of paying close attention to your line and pole tips, maintaining boat control and being patient.

Summary
Chapter 7 The Bite

>*Pole tips consistently spaced and about six inches above the water is perfect for detecting strikes.*

>*A quick hookset followed by light, steady pressure is best to bring a crappie to the top.*

>*Experience teaches the difference in a bite and bumping cover.*

Chapter 8

Hooking, Playing & Landing

-Setting the Hook
-Playing a Fish
-Landing a Crappie

Hooking, Playing and Landing

Setting the Hook

Setting the hook is a simple yet greatly abused technique. The long pole hookset is a moderately quick lift with the wrist. It must be firm enough to cause the hook to penetrate a crappie's mouth; even the bony upper lip. The hook setting must not continue after hook penetration or it will rip the hook out of the crappie's lips.

If a hook pops out of a fish played close to the boat, the hook set was too light. The same is true when a hook falls out after a fish is laid into the boat.

A hookup with a crappie followed immediately by losing the fish is a good indication that pressure applied was too much and/or too long.

As mentioned earlier, don't set the hook every time a pole moves. See if it's a stump or a bite. When you run into a stump, the pole tip will move slowly downward and opposite the direction the boat is going. In other words, if slow trolling forward, the pole will gradually bend toward the back of the boat.

The setting of a hook is something that comes from experience. Everything must be right but it's very simple and basic. Catching and losing fish is your best teacher.

Playing a Fish

Playing a crappie for fun should be done with an ultra-light outfit and casting techniques. A crappie can put up a real battle. Fast trolling with a lot of line out the back is another way to catch crappie.

Slow trolling is unlike casting and fast trolling. Vertical trolling is a get-him-in-the-boat technique. There's obviously a fight with a long pole, but it's limited to a vertical pull upward as quickly as possible.

A long pole will fight the fish for you. All you have to do is just keep mild pressure on the pole. It will provide a natural drag to absorb the shock while applying pressure to a fish.

Don't 'hoss' a crappie. Line breaks and ripped mouths are the result.

Steve says, "Slack line is the number one reason for lost fish. Constant, mild pressure is all that's needed to keep a line tight. Also, don't drop a pole tip to take up line. You'll lose the fish and you're sure to tangle your line at the pole tip."

If six poles are out and a fish is caught on a middle pole, how do you land the fish?

"By setting the hook, pulling the pole back about three feet and swinging the fish to the side of the boat under each pole," says Steve. "The other poles must be lifted one at a time with your free hand until the fish is worked past the poles placed back in their holders. You then have a fish that can be lifted into the boat or handled at the side of the boat."

Get a net to 'em quick! A big slab will go free if you give her slack line, pull too hard or try to lift her into the boat.

An example that's very common for working a pole to the side of the boat is when a big white bass or catfish is hooked. They can't be brought to the top quickly. If they remain positioned on a middle pole, they'll tangle every line at the front of the boat. Therefore, they must be worked away from other poles for fishing and landing.

Landing a Crappie

Small fish can be landed by swinging them into the boat. Big fish, probably any over a pound, should be netted. A big fish will rip itself off of the hook due to its weight. Also, light wire hooks can bend with a big fish in the air.

A net can be your personal choice. It should always stay in one handy location ready for quick use. Tournament fishermen should have a long handled net. Ronnie and Steve use a fourteen foot long net to give them access to any fish. "We've netted fish when the hook has already pulled out of the mouth. We've won tournaments with our net; Tom-Bigby is one example...he fell off in the net."

A big net mouth to get under a fish is good, too. However, the hole shouldn't be so big to cause the net to get in the way while in the boat. A little testing with a net will let you decide what is right for you.

Summary
Chapter 8 Hooking, Playing & Landing

>A quick wrist snap followed by constant soft pressure is all that's required for a hookset.

>A long pole acts like a drag to absorb shock. The pressure will cause the fish to come to the top.

>Slack line is the number one cause of lost fish.

>Net a big fish.

Chapter 9

Seasonal Patterns

-Spawn
-Post-Spawn
-Summer
-Fall/Winter
-Winter
-Early Spring

Seasonal Patterns

Seasonal changes are important for crappie fishermen to know and understand. Knowledge of patterns allow logical decisions to be made for areas to search. Although a detailed description would be much too lengthy for this book, a summary matches seasonal movements to slow vertical trolling.

Spawn

A lot of crappie go to the bank, especially during rising waters. It's the time of year when anyone can catch crappie by almost any method. The spawn is 'Crappie Season'.

Not all fish go to the bank, however. This is the Capps and Coleman philosophy. Some crappie spawn deep and those are the ones they're after. Ronnie explains, "There's no doubt about it. You can catch those big black males out there on the ledges in 15, 18 and 20 feet of water. They're building a nest up on top of a ledge."

Why go after the deep crappie instead of the shallow fish? More pounds. The fish are bigger although the bank may have more numbers.

"Slow vertical trolling works great for the deep fish, but shallow water fishermen can use it too. The perimeter of the bank can be trolled for shallow fish. We've done this when the wind would get too high to fish deep, open water."

Post-Spawn

"It's common to catch fish in the same places as in the spawn. Fish are often finicky and we catch fewer fish. One thing to note is that once a particular piece of cover is found to hold fish, you will probably catch more numbers in post-spawn than you will during the spawn."

Summer

The technique doesn't change in the summer. The biggest difference is that a thermocline may set up.

A thermocline is a quick change in water temperature at a particular depth. The fish will be on or above the thermocline in 'sweet' water. Temperatures, pH and oxygen levels below the thermocline aren't suited for active fish.

There are three simple ways to find a thermocline. First, the majority of the fish will be at or above the cline. For example, crappie will stack at 11 to 15 feet in 30 feet of water. You can see them on your locator. This would likely indicate a thermocline at 15 feet.

Another indication is dying minnows. Minnows die quickly when placed below the thermocline. If the minnow is alive at 13 feet but dead when dropped to 16 feet it indicates a definite cline.

A third method is to use a meter to check for a rapid temperature and pH level change.

Ronnie and Steve have good luck catching fish in hot weather but they may have to search a while. In shallow lakes like Reelfoot, the fish move around a lot and many go to very shallow water. Therefore, you should keep an open mind when searching for summer crappie. If they're not in your favorite spots, don't hesitate to move.

Fall/Early Winter

Fall fish will start moving slowly toward deeper water as it gets cold. It's actually the reverse of early spring fishing. Fish are easier to catch once they are found. Stick to basics. Fish cover along ledges.

Seasonal patterns move fish to different locations.
It's critical to use a good topo map when searching for fish.

Winter

A good tactic for deep winter fishing is 'extremely slow' vertical trolling. "Fish need a slow bait; slower than other seasons. That's funny because it's the best fishing of the year. The fish are anxious to bite and it's the best grade of fish of the year," says Ronnie.

Early Spring

The key water temperature for finding, formulating a pattern and catching good numbers of quality fish is 59 degrees. Below 59 degrees keeps the fish active yet stable. Above 59 degrees they start to roam, scatter and move day to day. This is good for a weekend angler trying to catch some fish but it's terrible for a fisherman looking for a deep water pattern.

Summary
Chapter 9 Seasonal Patterns

>*Finding fish requires that a fisherman knows seasonal fish movements.*

>*Slow trolling works in the spring even though the majority of fish goes shallow.*

>*Stay above the summer thermocline.*

>*Slow down when water is cold.*

Chapter 10

Fishing the Elements

>Wind
>Strong Wind
>Bad Wind
>More on Wind
>Rising/High Water
>Current
>Fishing Pressure
>Sunlight
>Clear Water
>Muddy Water

The Elements

Facing tough weather and water conditions is part of fishing. Knowing when, where and how to handle bad situations is what separates many of the good fishermen. Trying new tactics,

remembering what does and doesn't work and going the extra mile to do what's necessary to put fish into the boat makes a fishermen much better.

What do you do when the water is high and muddy? There are no guaranteed solutions but the following are a few experiences of Ronnie and Steve. Maybe some of their knowledge can be applied to your style of fishing.

Wind

No other condition can be worse than high wind. It's not enjoyable to fish in the wind. Efficiency decreases with bouncing poles, slack line and additional boat control problems. The worst problem is safety.

Winds can occur during any season, but spring is the most likely time. The following is a list of tested ideas for solving wind problems. You might use them the next time you're faced with windy conditions. Keep safety a top priority.

(1) The first, simplest and most obvious solution is to have different areas around the lake to fish. You should find a wind break no matter which direction the wind is from. If you get a hard north wind, you should have at least one or two areas along northern banks for wind protection.

The key to fishing in wind is to pay close attention to the weather forecast. It will help in selecting the right areas and let you know how to prepare.

(2) The second idea is to add weight to bait rigs. A bouncing bait is the worst problem in the wind. Switching from a 1/2-ounce to a 3/4-ounce egg sinker will keep baits stationary. Less bounce means more bites.

Weight also keeps lines more vertical in case you're suddenly caught moving too fast. Light sinkers take a lot longer to get back down when lines move out to a 45 degree angle.

(3) Always fish into the wind. Going against the wind is a requirement for positioning. Why not go with the wind? If you go with the wind, you can't stop the boat when you find fish or get a bite. You're right over and past the good area before it is properly fished. When two or three poles hang up in the brush, you'll delay fishing for a while to tie on new rigs.

Strong Winds

(4) "It's gotten so rough that we've had to hold our poles to know what was happening," says Steve. Holding poles buffers the bounce of baits giving more bites. Bites can be felt and the hook set.

The disadvantage of holding poles is a limit of two poles per fisherman. One pole must be immediately put into a holder when a fish hits the other pole.

(5) The fifth idea for wind is to add weight. Ronnie and Steve like to put as much weight as possible in the front of the boat. It's really important to them. Gas cans, batteries and anything else heavy is added to the front of the boat. This does one important thing. It reduces the amount of bounce that the front of the boat will have. Therefore, baits are more stationary and the fishermen are more comfortable.

Bad Winds: Extreme Limits

Note: The following ideas are not promoted by this author. Observe all safety precautions while on the water. The following are tricks of the pros for catching crappie.

Extreme conditions call for extreme measures. Common sense and staying at home might be the best choice. Sometimes fishing in tournaments requires that adjustments be made and limits pushed. It's important to know that the following information are not recommendations, but rather what has worked for Ronnie and Steve. Stay within all safety limits of your boat and use common sense.

(6) "We have used concrete blocks in the boat to add weight. Another method is to add big rocks like rip-rap. These let us add as much weight as we want and more importantly, it can be gotten rid of quickly in case the boat fills up with water," says Ronnie.

(7) Another method of theirs is to fill the boat with water. This method adds stability. It adds weight and therefore reduces bounce. Secondly, it puts the boat down into the water for a lower profile. A low profile means less boat exposure to be caught by the wind.

There are many disadvantages to adding weight. Too much weight means that safety limits of the boat will be exceeded. It also means that wind conditions are very bad. High waves and swells can enter the boat and swamp it. Experience along with common sense should be used in weight addition.

(8) An alternative idea for serious fishermen who are going to fish the wind is to add a kicker motor. On a previous boat, Ronnie and Steve built a bracket so they could add a trolling motor next to their left front seat. This position allowed them to steer and control speed.

Ronnie says, "We often have two trolling motors pulling us when it gets real windy. We leave the one on the side on all of the time. The extra motor holds us in a neutral position. The main motor is for control. It's hard to fish with two motors because it's a little extra work. The wind is whipping and a large wave is coming over the bow now and then. The bilge pump is usually working overtime. Everything has to be happening at the same time."

(9) Another tournament trick is to fish from the back of the boat. The back of the boat is wider, heavier and more stable.

Steve explains, "We like to fish into a ledge, not off of it. If the wind is blowing into a ledge, Ronnie stays in front and holds the boat with the trolling motor. I fish off the back of the boat on the ledge." Steve's responsibility is to catch fish while Ronnie controls the boat. This is an excellent example of teamwork.

(10) Drag a chain. The reason a chain works so well is that it seldom gets hung up. A chain will roll and climb over a rock or log where an anchor will grab. This method is the only way Ronnie and Steve will go 'with' the wind.

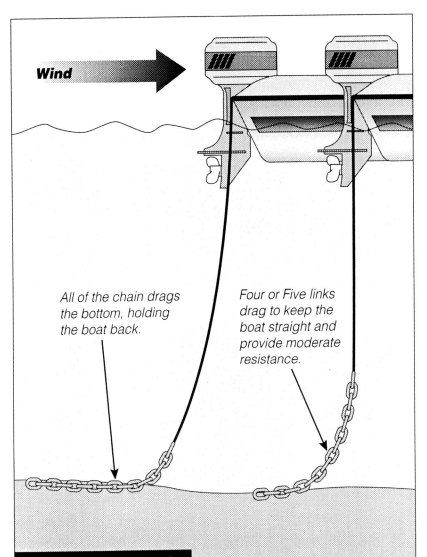

Wind

All of the chain drags the bottom, holding the boat back.

Four or Five links drag to keep the boat straight and provide moderate resistance.

Dragging a Chain

Extremely hard wind makes boat control impossible. Changing tactics by letting a chain drag behind the boat does two important things. First, it slows the boat down. Second, it keeps it straight. Speed and control are important elements for catching crappie.

"We have a logging chain that weights about twenty-five pounds. There's something about a chain when it hits a bottom of mud or silt. These's a lot of friction and it really grabs," says Ronnie. The chain is connected to a rope and is hung vertically out of the back of the boat.

"Adjust until you get gust the right speed. We change it by letting it in or out and then tying-off the rope. Letting an additional 4 or 5 links drag can make a very big difference. A pulley system on back with a control switch in front would be an ideal setup."

This works in deep or shallow water. The team has used it at Kentucky Lake in deep water and on Reelfoot Lake in shallows. It helped them win the Reelfoot Lake tournament a few years ago.

"A lot of people use a chain almost like an anchor. They'll throw it out and move only when a hard just of wind hits them. They might work a small area of stumps taking an hour to fish through them."

A chain is heavy and messy. A plastic coating or something slick to let the mud come off with ease would be an advantage. However, the weight and mess are worthwhile if you want to fish a particular stretch of water in the wind.

More On Wind

Think ahead. Plan your areas and have the items in your boat needed for windy conditions.

The worst situation for bad wind is for it to come up after it has been calm especially when it's not predicted. This type of wind will ruin your fishing and can be extremely dangerous to smaller boats on large waters.

Wind doesn't change the mood of fish very much, according to Ronnie and Steve. They basically stay on the same fishing pattern. However, in shallow water, waves can muddy up your fishing area.

Rising/High Water

Rising water can be a slow, moderate to very fast rise. A moderate rise will probably include a little more current in creeks and rivers along with a tint (mud stain) in some inlet areas. The rise will be on the tail end of a strong frontal system.

Ronnie has made a unique finding on a rise and high water. "Most people think that all crappie move shallow in high water. It's true for the crappie around the bank. They get incredibly shallow. Fish in deep water are different. They'll stay the same or go deeper."

The team stays on the same structure they were fishing before the rise. It will be deeper after a rise. From there, they search deeper and shallower until they find the fish. Crappie will usually be deeper.

All presentations for the deep crappie remain the same.

Current

Fish will be less active in strong current. They'll move right up against the structure. They'll always face the current.

Ronnie explains. "Fish will sometimes stay in the current. In bad current they'll move. In a river system, I'd recommend trying to find other fish."

The team used this knowledge and a little logic to win a Kentucky Lake Crappiethon USA tournament. They had been catching huge slabs in the main channel. Rains came a week before the tournament causing currents to rapidly increase. They knew the big fish wouldn't stay in the main river, so they searched just outside the current in the mouth of a bay. The fish had been pushed into the slack water and were bunched on a point. Solving the puzzle paid big dividends with enough big fish to win the tournament.

The team was fishing in the Crappie USA 1997 Classic on Truman Lake, Missouri and was again faced with an unusual condition. Rain caused tough conditions and high water. On day two of the tournament they needed ten good fish to take the win. When they got to the creek that had produced well the day before they were disappointed in what they found.

Ronnie and Steve said that water was coming out of the creek so fast they could hardly get in it. It was gushing out. Water fell at least a foot so it was sucking out of that creek.

Steve says, "Water was muddy with current. That gave us an advantage in that we didn't have to fish the whole trees today; just the back side where fish were getting out of the current."

"We caught twenty fish yesterday and thirteen today."

Ronnie says, "The fish were unbelievably sluggish. We had to hold the bait there for 30 seconds sometimes. It wasn't a strike, it was just one of those 'get out of here' things. That's why we didn't get some of our best fish in today. They didn't want it. It was mental stress today because we knew we needed at least ten decent fish to win and we only had six fish before noon."

The boat positioning was horrible due to the wind. It was blowing the opposite direction of the current so they had to position on the upcurrent side of the trees and fish on the downcurrent side behind the trees.

Pickwick Lake last year (2002) was a good example. When they started pulling heavy current I found that if I could get on a protected area on a creek bed like a point where the channel bended back, the fish would stack up in that area. It was a place where current was less. The stretch of creek from one point to another on the down-current side would be good.

Again, the moral is to adjust to the wind and current. Fishing probably won't be better but you can make the best of a bad situation.

Trolling is an outstanding method for slowly presenting baits to sluggish fish in currents. Cover can be bumped with baits and the presentation provides plenty of time for a crappie to hit. This is just another positive aspect of slow vertical trolling.

Fishing Pressure

"This technique is a good method when fishing pressure is high. The method we use keeps our baits in the strike zone all of the time. Other fishermen aren't a problem."

Fast trollers have some problem in pressured areas because they can't stop moving. They quickly leave a good spot and they must turn abound and come back to go through it again. Pressured areas are likely to have boats go immediately to the spot where they see a fish caught.

Slow vertical trolling lets a fisherman ease around other boats. When brush and/or crappie are found, the spot can be thoroughly fished before continuing on. "We can't and don't worry about other boats. We've made circles around others and caught fish. We'll catch more fish with our method unless fish are really scattered."

Sunlight

"In real sunny conditions we've found that fish will be relating much tighter to cover than on cloudy days," says Ronnie. "They like to hide just like a bass. They're likely to be close to structure."

Two prime examples can be seen in two very different tournaments. The 1995 Crappiethon Classic in Ohio followed a day of drizzle and rain. A strong front passed through early on tournament morning. Early in the morning Ronnie and Steve caught fish relatively shallow in about 12 feet of water. By the end of the day they were catching crappie at 20 feet. Sunlight drove the fish deep.

"Dark conditions will cause the fish to be shallow. At Conway, Arkansas, we watched crappie striking minnows on top of the water early in the morning. Later in the day we were catching fish in the deepest part of the lake."

Clear Water

Ronnie and Steve have had some success fishing super-clear water, but they prefer not to fish in it if there is an option. Ronnie says, "At Cave Run Lake in Kentucky we could see a pop-top at 12 feet. I pay very close attention to structure in this type of lake. You're not likely to catch a fish away from structure and cover."

The team gets really slow and concentrates on putting baits directly into the cover. Slow presentation speeds along with thick cover are the keys. Something different is also important. "We got on a buck brush pattern at Cave Run. Where the brush was thickest we did okay."

Shallow, clear water is probably the worst enemy of slow vertical trolling. Spooking fish can be a problem. Switching to 18 to 20 foot long poles and ultra-light line helps to eliminate some of the problems.

Muddy Water

The team considers two types of mud conditions. The first is mud in shallow areas caused by wind. They avoid these areas when possible. They have not had good luck catching fish in shallow, windblown muddy water.

The second type of mud is better but not good. Natural mud or mud due to rain is not really that much different from each other; they both cause fish to scatter," says Ronnie.

"An extremely important tournament mind-set is to not prejudge a lake with mixed conditions. Both a muddy area of the lake and a clearer portion of the lake are equal until fished. Only after fishing both locations will a muddy water/clear water decision be made."

"If I had my choice, I'd like a little clearer water. That's because there will be more fish associated to particular cover and structure as opposed to being scattered in muddy water. However, an example of how fish can be caught in muddy water was at Tom-Bigby. We got on a stump flat but the fish weren't on cover. They were out in the open. We won Pickwick the same way after a flood."

Summary
Chapter 10 Fishing the Elements

>In the wind, add weight to bait rigs and maintain boat control.

>In cold water or really bad wind, go with the wind and drag a chain.

>Fish the backside of structure when current is strong.

>Ultra-clear water is tough fishing. Use long 20-ft poles and look for cover where fish will be concentrated.

>Muddy water can still produce fish.

Chapter 11

Tournament Notes

Tournament Notes

The following are a few notes from the 1996 tournament season. They have been condensed to concentrate on the mood of the tournaments and the how-to tips you can learn from their experiences.

A tournament rule change to eight poles per team has been made since the 1996 season. You'll note that the team used many poles when limits were not in force.

Since 1996 season, this team has won the Crappie USA Classic Championship in 1997 and the NACA Championship Tournament in 2000.

Feb. 11, 1996

The team had just returned from a grueling trip from Florida. After a 12-hour drive, Ronnie called as he had promised.

"Man, I'm tickled. We had good luck; so we've decided to go ahead and make a run in the Pro Division (Zodiac point championship).

Weather?

"The weather was beautiful. They had just gotten off a cold snap. It was warm. I got sunburned."

Pre-fishing?

"We arrived Thursday around noon. We fished Carlton and quickly caught fish including a 1.2 and 1.5 pound fish."

"Friday we went to Dora and Griffin. We caught good average sized fish, but no really big ones. The most important things we learned was that Carlton still held the bigger fish and the fish moved from right on bottom at 13 feet up to 6 or 8 feet. That saved us some fish on tournament day."

Tournament day?

"It started kind of funny. You had to have a flashlight to bait your hook. It was totally dark at 6:30 am in Florida. It was foggy, too. That didn't help. We caught seven or eight (in the dark) but I don't think any of them weighed."

A team celebration following their first Classic championship at Ceasars Creek, Ohio. They quieted the rumors that they needed twenty poles to win a tournament...by fishing two poles apiece and beating the northern fishermen on their home waters.

"We caught fish all day long. We used our double-hook spread rigs. Everything was hitting on the top hook so we raised the bottom hook to about 10 feet and started catching fish on both hooks. Our biggest fish came around 9 o'clock. It was 1.78-lb."

We trolled sink holes on the east one direction and west coming back. It was a 400 yard stretch with a series of sink holes. No fish were in the holes."

"The holes were easy to find. Air bubbles were coming up. That confused some people because those bubbles showed on the LCR as fish. But all of the fish were on the edge of the drop at 13 feet dropping to around 18. The crappie on tournament day were suspended over the drops."

Did you make any adjustments during the day?

"Yes we did. I read an article where a guide said that glow jigs were good. Steve had four poles out the back that he used glow heads on including some Southern Pro Slow Fall heads. Steve added a Lit'l Hustler skirt and minnow."

"The jig was very light and would barely sink. With our slow trolling and putting the baits about 22 yards behind the boat, they stayed about 6 or 8 feet deep. Those four poles caught at least four of the fish that we weighed in."

How many poles did you fish?

"I fished 9 long poles in holders while casting to my left with another. Steve ran 12 double rigs and 4 spinning outfits with the glow jigs. I guess we fished 26 poles all day."

Any tips for fishing there?

"It was important to pay attention. The fish had to be hit quick when they hit. Fishermen should be ready to strike as soon as they see a bite."

Any bad experiences?

"Like other fishermen, we lost one that would have won the tournament. Steve was coming with the net. It flashed and came off the top hook. I hooked it again when the bottom hook shot up and snagged it. But I only came out of the water with a scale. That fish would have easily won us the tournament."

March 3

"We put some practice time in last week. We found fish in the deepest water in the lake. The lake is shallow over-all but it has some 25 foot water where old lakes were when it was flooded. Three of these held good fish," says Ronnie about Ross Barnett Lake in Mississippi.

"Thursday and Friday weren't good practice days. The fish had moved. We looked in a lot of places. We went up the main channel and found some females."

Tournament day?

"It was tough. We started by fishing two and a half hours with no good fish. We moved to Steve's spot and fished another hour and a half with no fish. We couldn't believe it didn't produce. Then we kept going up the river. It was something we didn't prefish."

"The wind got up. We caught one good fish and then another about thirty minutes later. We sunk the boat so we could stay in the spot and fish. By sinking I mean that we plugged the livewell and kept pumping water. We had enough water in the boat that the fish were swimming upright in the floor. It weighted our boat and set us down out of the wind a little. It kept our baits still."

"We caught twice our limit probably but just kept the big ones. We were proud we won. It was a tough day."

March 10

How did the tournament go at Santee Cooper, SC?

"We almost froze to death. I've never been so cold crappie fishing. It was 15 degrees and only got to about freezing."

"Prefishing was terrible. The lakes were white capping so bad. Steve tore everything up Thursday when he came early to prefish. He tried to fish some but the wind was bad."

The tournament was a peculiar day because the weather was miserable yet the best one-day tournament weight was beaten not by one team, but all of the top ten or twenty teams.

How did your fishing go?

"The day was terribly cold. We had to stay in Whaybo Swamp to fish because of the wind."

"We did everything like we always do. We found fish so we stayed with them. We culled to improve our stringer. I thought we were in it until I got to the weight-in line. I had no idea there wee crappie that big in the lake. I was embarrassed. However, I'm sure we could have won the 'white' crappie tournament."

March 30

It has been a few weeks since I've talked to the team. Weiss Lake was a tough tournament for the team but they did catch fish.

"Steve fished Eufaula AL/GA tournament by himself. He caught tons of fish and did a good job, but never got the good ones to hit."

Pickwick, AL/TN/MS. "This past weekend we were at Pickwick. We didn't prefish. We finished sixth."

"Conditions at Pickwick included rising water and 53 degrees. We tried fishing deep in Bear Creek. It was warm and calm so we moved a little more shallow as the day progressed. We were a little disappointed we didn't catch some really big fish, but 14.5 pounds wasn't too bad."

"We had something kind of odd happen. Current was noticeable so fish were tight to cover. I bumped one stump and had nine poles to go down. We caught all nine fish and they were good ones. It was over in thirty seconds. We didn't get another bite. I guess we caught all of the fish that were on that stump."

April 6

Interview at Kentucky Lake following the tourney. "I was into some real good fish while practicing," says Steve. "But the fish were in four foot waves today, so we just went back to where we caught some two years ago. There are some big crappie in there. We caught a couple over two pounds and one just under three (2.96-lbs). We were lucky because we did not prefish the spot."

How about the points race? You and Ronnie are in hot pursuit of the championship along with Wayne and Barry Bunch and a few others. (At the beginning of the year Ronnie and Steve were planning to fish six tournaments.)

"We'll fish every weekend (twelve tournaments) and try to win the points division."

It's early April. Any tips for fishermen at this time of year?

Here's a huge slab taken during a Kentucky Lake tournament.

"Suspended fish are difficult to catch but right now you've got the migration going on in the big bays and sloughs. When they're going they'll get on the bottom and on stumps," explains Steve.

"They're associated with structure, but they suspend up. These we caught today were associated with a sand bar. The big one hit slow. He was barely hooked, but we had the net ready."

April 13

Kentucky Lake north: today they win. The team has two 1st place and two 2nd place finishes in tournaments averaging around 160 teams per tournament. The front cover of this book was taken today at the weigh-in site.

How did you fish?

Ronnie says, "We were in real shallow water at about 9 to 11 feet. We were in the very upper end of a river."

"We worked a little creek ledge that has a 1.5-foot drop. We trolled 500 to 600 yards. We caught about 50-percent on minnows and the other on Umbrella tube jigs."

"We had a delay and had to leave for over two hours when the storm came through. We went back where we won last week and never caught a fish."

"The wind settled and we came back. We had seven fish in about the first 45 minutes this morning that were tournament fish. They were really there. When the storm hit we were still catching fish. We left and came back. They had quit biting but the one crappie we did catch weighed 2.68 so it worked out."

Why did you fish shallow?

"Yesterday," says Steve, "I fished and didn't have anywhere to fish because of the wind. I went back as far as I could go into shallow water and found it to be two degrees warmer. I immediately caught one that weighed 2.10 and caught another exactly like it. I turned around and floated off knowing that's where we would fish this morning."

You've finished 1st and 2nd at the two Kentucky Lake tournaments. How about next week?

"It's Grand Lake of the Cherokees. We've never seen it. I'm going to drive there on Thursday and prefish Friday."

One Week Later

"Tim, it was awful," explains Ronnie. "We tied for 4th in the Minn Kota division. The fishing was pitiful. We caught ten fish and were lucky to do that. They were under the docks." (Where Ronnie and Steve couldn't get).

The lake was clear. It was too clear to troll. We had to go to the brush. There were no steep drops and few brush piles."

April 27

Beaver Lake, Arkansas. Ronnie, "I picked War Eagle because of its fertility. I knew White River was a cold clear river

Some nice Truman Lake, MO crappie taken during a Crappie USA tournament.

Receiving their awards for the 1997 National Championship by
winning the Crappie USA Classic at Truman Lake, MO.
(L to R) Jim Perry, board member; Ronnie Capps, champ;
Wayne Wolf, corporate sponsor rep.; Steve Coleman, champ;
Steve McCadams, board member;
Darrell Van Vactor, president/ceo Crappie USA.

and that's not prime for crappie. What I saw in War Eagle was
what I liked. I talked to locals and they confirmed there were some
good ones in there."

"I spent Thursday running forty gallons of gas looking
elsewhere. Just looking. I fished Joe and and a couple of others and
caught small fish. Brushy wasn't bad but it was cold."

"On Friday I concentrated in War Eagle and caught some really nice ones. I caught some monsters, but they were post-spawn and skinny."

How did you catch fish today during the tournament?

"It was simple. A creek bend with a ledge, 17 feet at the bottom and 12 feet on top. A classic spot."

"Today we caught about 40 keepers."

The team finished 3rd.

May 12

Last week it was tough catching crappie at Mississinew Salamonie, IN. The team caught a few small fish in practice but didn't catch any on tournament day.

Yesterday at Monroe, IN the team came back to win the tournament. It was interesting how they beat 200 other teams.

"The fish were in pre-spawn," says Ronnie. "We tried something a little different on Friday. The lake was really high. Steve took the boat and I took a canoe. The purpose was to locate fish, deep or shallow."

"I couldn't believe it when I pulled into the first flooded blackberry thicket. My pole doubled with a good fish. While I was taking that one off another one was trying to get to my jig that was just dangling a few inches in the water. It was really wild. I kept a few just show Steve. Four were monsters."

"We got close with the big boat on tournament day and anchored the big boat. We used the canoe to fish. The key was the blackberry thickets on the edge of pastures. The water was 15 feet high. The fish had moved into the bushes where the sun was shining. We caught dozens of big crappie. It was a special day."

They set a new Monroe tournament record by catching ten fish weighing 16.14 pounds.

June 4,5,6

The Crappiethon USA Classic, Lake Chickamauga, Chattanooga, TN. Ronnie and Steve were invited back as the defending champions. However, they had qualified on many lakes and would have been there anyway.

Classic Practice Day

It started out bad when they didn't get the wake-up call to their room. They had to throw on their clothes, skip breakfast and head to the lake.

The first spot they fished was great. They caught several good fish in just a few minutes. The rest of the day was spent searching for better locations. None were found.

The team had an excellent attitude that night. They believed that within all of the decent fish they found would be some good kickers to give them an excellent shot at the title. The only regret they had was not making the long trip to the Hiwassii where they knew some quality fish should be located. Time would tell.

Classic Day

The weather changed. A strong front moved through early in the morning and dropped rain throughout the day. Conditions changed the crappie's aggressiveness and depths. Many fishermen struggled.

Ronnie and Steve at the Grenada Lake Classic

Fishing was slow for Ronnie and Steve. I watched them from a distance but the good crappie of yesterday weren't biting very often. A lot of little ones and a few decent fish were all they had caught within the first hour.

The day continued much the same for the team. They continued to catch a good average fish mixed with a lot of small ones. The two or three big kicker slabs they had hoped for didn't come, but their average fish were very good for the conditions.

Weigh-in was exciting. Out of 150 of the best crappie teams in the country, Ronnie and Steve finished third with 9.13-lbs.

"I wouldn't have done anything different," says Ronnie. "We checked a ledge and was very fortunate that they were there. Past knowledge helped me a lot and I felt pretty good coming up here."

"After locating fish we were real confident. There was another place that turned out to be better than ours. We knew there was a good chance of that."

TOURNAMENTS
Ronnie Capps & Steve Coleman

>More than a dozen national qualifier **tournaments wins**

>**Team-of-the-Year Titles**
     1992 Crappiethon Pro Division Championship.
     1996 Crappiethon Zodiac Points Championship

>**Classic Wins**
     1995 Crappiethon USA Ceasars Creek, OH
     1997 Crappie USA at Truman Lake, MO
     2000 NACA at Ross Barnnett, MS

Summary
Chapter 11 Tournament Notes

>*A quick net can save a big crappie that's poorly hooked.*

>*You don't need a big drop-off to find crappie. A 1.5-ft drop held big fish for Ronnie and Steve to give them another tournament win.*

>*If visiting a new lake, look for the most fertile water.*

>*Really high water gives new covers you should try. A blackberry patch held big fish for a tournament win up north.*

>*Be patient with an area you know holds good fish.*

Appendix

The Miscellaneous Stuff

Slow Trolling Equipment
used by Capps & Coleman

Boat: Ranger

Liquid Crystal Graph: Lowrance

GPS: Lowrance

Trolling Motor: Minn Kota 101

Maps: Geological; HotSpots

Pole Holders: Lok-Tite

Poles: BnM

Reels: Mitchell

Line: Berkley Trilene

Hook: Eagle Claw 214EL #2

Sinker: Egg

Bait: Minnows

Bait: Southern Pro jigs

Photos of Other Slow Trollers

Photos of Other Slow Trollers

Photos of Other Slow Trollers

Photos of Other Slow Trollers

Bladder Pressure Relief

Pressure changes in air can cause physical reactions. This is why fish change water depths when strong fronts move though. Crappie want to stay comfortable. An air bladder needs to maintain equalization.

What makes a crappie lay on its side and often die when pulled from deep water?

Steve Coleman says, "When you catch one deep and pull it up, it chokes. The stomach goes into its throat."

Steve compares the reaction to that of a Coke bottle. A plastic bottle can be dropped to 33 feet, filled to normal size with air, then brought to the top; it will explode. That's similar to what happens to the air sac in a fish.

The solution is to release the air from the fish. "We use a medium size hypodermic needle. A small one won't work. We find the air sack by running a finger straight down to the lateral line under the third or fourth spine of the dorsal fin (top fin). The sack is easy to feel; like a big knot. We angle the needle at a 45 degree angle to the sac, let the air out and pull the needle. The 45 degree angle lets us get under the scales easier and when we pull the needle out, the scales fall back over the hole. The fish isn't damaged; he's in better condition."

Special Thanks

Ronnie & Steve. Several fishing trips and many telephone interviews were required for the first book and more interviews when this revised edition was written. Their time and patience for photos, answering questions and describing their technique is appreciated.

Fishing HotSpots for permission to use portions of their contour maps within Winning Crappie Secrets. For information concerning top quality contour fishing maps or to get the book "Catch Fish with Maps" call: FHS Maps: 1-800-ALL-MAPS.

To God who has provided a way for my eternal life. He has blessed me in many ways including a wonderful wife and the opportunity to be outdoors to enjoy nature, watch beautiful sunrises, catch a few crappie and to write about what I have learned. Life is good thanks to Him.

Contacts

Steve Coleman is available for a limited number of guide trips on Reelfoot Lake and Kentucky Lake. Phone 731-253-7148

Ronnie Capps guides for duck hunting on Reelfoot Lake and has a hunting video available. www.reelfootsecrets.com This video is a quality, high-tech, 21st century how-to for duck hunting.

Boyette's Resort (at Reelfoot Lake) www.lakereelfoot.net
Rt 1, Box 1230, Tiptonville, TN 38079
731-253-6523; 1-888-465-6523 for reservations
(also has Reelfoot Secrets duck hunting video available for sale)

Crappie Info & Tournaments

CRAPPIE World magazine is the best crappie publication available. It's packed with how-to features, where-to-go lake profiles and tons of good fishing information. 1-800-554-1999.

Crappie USA/American Crappie Association offers the premier national crappie tournament circuit along with an association open to tournament and non-tournament fishermen. Has a quarterly magazine...Crappie Journal. 1-888-311-CUSA or www.crappieusa.com.

North American Crappie Association (NACA) has a national tournament trial; magazine. 870-931-7152 or www.northamericancrappie.com

Crappie Anglers Sportsman's Tour (CAST) has a national tournament trail. 913-322-2919 or www.castamerica.com

More from Huffman Publishing

Seasonal Structures for Crappie

Released Jan 1998; 180+ pages; soft cover, $9.50

This book is based upon the CRAPPIE World Magazine column, Seasonal Structures. The book gives many fish-catching tips and tactics. It makes catching crappie easier by matching the type structure to season, tactics and the best presentations.

Grizzly Fishin' for Bluegill (also includes crappie & Reelfoot Lake)

Released Feb 2001; 64 pages; soft cover, $6.50

Here's an ultralight jigging method that's easy to use and will catch many different species.

"The advantage of the Grizzly Fishin' technqiue is that it turns an average fisherman into a very good fisherman."...Louie Mansfield.

Monster Crappie

Released Aug 2002; 128 pages; 60+ photos; soft cover; $9.50

Written for one purpose...to give tips and tactics for catching bigger crappie. Trolling crankbaits, wade fishing and power trolling are the three featured techniques but other tactics are included, too.

This book can be your guide to catching that wall-hanger you've always dreamed of landing. An outline and top lakes will help get you started right.

www.monstercrappie.com

To order, send name, address and check or money order. Special autographed copies, gifts or other requests welcomed.

Prices include shipping and handling:

Winning Crappie Secrets $11.50
Seasonal Structure for Crappie $11.50
Grizzly Fishin' $7.50
Monster Crappie $11.50

Huffman Publishing, PO Box 26, Poplar Bluff, MO 63902-0026